F.V.

WITHDRAWN

SONINKE

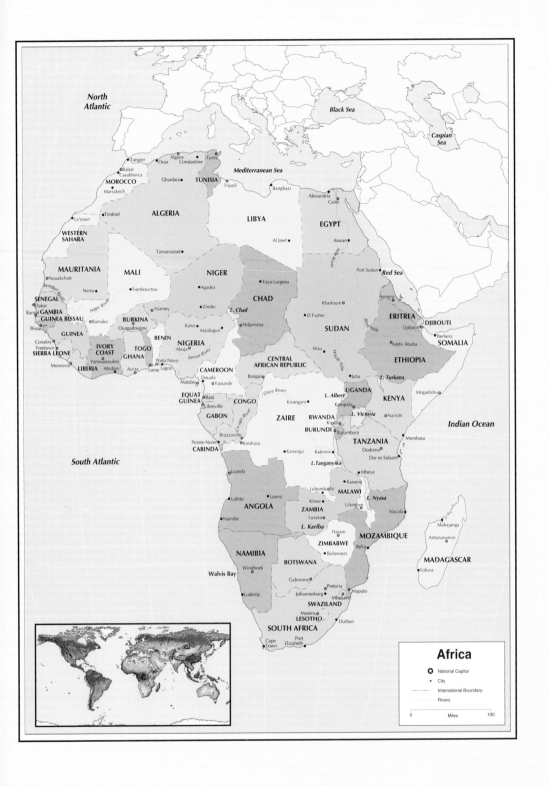

North
Atlantic

Black Sea

Caspian
Sea

Tangier
Rabat
Casablanca
MOROCCO
Marrakech

Algiers
Oran Constantine
Ghardaia

Tunis
TUNISIA

Mediterranean Sea

Tripoli

Banghazi

Alexandria
Cairo

La'youn
Tindouf

ALGERIA

LIBYA

EGYPT

WESTERN
SAHARA

Al Jawf

Aswan

Tamanrasset

Port Sudan   Red Sea

MAURITANIA
Nouakchott

MALI

NIGER

Faya-Largeau

Asmera
ERITREA

Nema

Tombouctou

Agadez

CHAD

Khartoum

El Fasher

Djibouti   DJIBOUTI
Berbera
SOMALIA

SENEGAL
Dakar
Banjul GAMBIA
GUINEA BISSAU
Bissau
Conakry
Freetown
SIERRA LEONE
Monrovia
LIBERIA

Niger River
Bamako
Ouagadougou
BURKINA
GUINEA
IVORY
COAST
Yamoussoukro
Abidjan

Niamey
Zinder
L. Chad
Kano
Maidugun
BENIN
NIGERIA
Abuja
TOGO
GHANA   Porto Novo
Accra Lome Lagos

Ndjamena

Wau

SUDAN

White Nile
Blue Nile

Addis Ababa

ETHIOPIA

CENTRAL
AFRICAN REPUBLIC

Bangui

Juba

L. Turkana

Mogadishu

CAMEROON
Douala
Malabo   Yaounde
EQUAT
GUINEA   Bata
Libreville
GABON

(Zaire River)

CONGO

Kisangani

L. Albert
UGANDA

Kampala
L. Victoria

KENYA

Nairobi

Indian Ocean

Congo River

ZAIRE

RWANDA
Kigali
BURUNDI   Bujumbura

Brazzaville
Pointe-Noire
CABINDA
Kinshasa

South Atlantic

Kananga

Kalemie

L.Tanganyika

TANZANIA
Dodoma
Dar es Salaam

Mombasa

Luanda

Lobito   Luena

Mbeya

Lubumbashi
Kitwe
MALAWI
Kasama

L. Nyasa

ANGOLA
Namibe

ZAMBIA
Lusaka
L. Kariba

Lilongwe

Nacala

Mahajanga
Antananarivo

Harare
ZIMBABWE
Bulawayo
Belra

MOZAMBIQUE

MADAGASCAR
Toliara

NAMIBIA
Windhoek

BOTSWANA

Walvis Bay

Gaborone

Luderitz

Johannesburg
Pretoria
Mbabane
SWAZILAND
Maseru
LESOTHO   Durban
SOUTH AFRICA
Cape   Port
Town   Elizabeth

Maputo

0   Miles   100

Africa

⊛   National Capital

•   City

- - -   International Boundary

      Rivers

The Heritage Library of African Peoples

SONINKE

C. O. Nwanunobi, Ph.D.

THE ROSEN PUBLISHING GROUP, INC.
NEW YORK

Published in 1996 by The Rosen Publishing Group, Inc.
29 East 21st Street, New York, NY 10010

First Edition

Manufactured in the United States of America

Library of Congress Cataloging-in-Publication Data

Nwanunobi, C.
    Soninke / C. Nwanunobi. — 1st ed.
      p. cm. — (The heritage library of African peoples)
    Includes bibliographical references and index.
    ISBN 0-8239-1978-1
    1. Soninke (African people)—History—Juvenile literature.
  2. Soninke (African people)—Social life and customs—Juvenile
literature. [1. Soninke (African people)] I. Title. II. Series.
DT549.45.S66N93   1995
966—dc20   94-45813
                                      CIP
                                       AC

Contents

INTRODUCTION

THERE IS EVERY REASON FOR US TO KNOW
something about Africa and to understand its
past and the way of life of its peoples. Africa is a
rich continent that has for centuries provided
the world with art, culture, labor, wealth, and
natural resources. It has vast mineral deposits,
fossil fuels, and commercial crops.

But perhaps most important is the fact that
fossil evidence indicates that human beings
originated in Africa. The earliest traces of
human beings and their tools are almost two
million years old. Their descendants have
migrated throughout the world. To be human is
to be of African descent.

The experiences of the peoples who stayed in
Africa are as rich and as diverse as of those who
established themselves elsewhere. This series of
books describes their environment, their modes
of subsistence, their relationships, and their customs and beliefs. The books present the variety
of languages, histories, cultures, and religions
that are to be found on the African continent.
They demonstrate the historical linkages between
African peoples and the way contemporary Africa
has been affected by European colonial rule.

Africa is large, complex, and diverse. It en-
compasses an area of more than 11,700,000

square miles. The United States, Europe, and India could fit easily into it. The sheer size is an indication of the continent's great variety in geography, terrain, climate, flora, fauna, peoples, languages, and cultures.

Much of contemporary Africa has been shaped by European colonial rule, industrialization, urbanization, and the demands of a world economic system. For more than seventy years, large regions of Africa were ruled by Great Britain, France, Belgium, Portugal, and Spain. African peoples from various ethnic, linguistic, and cultural backgrounds were brought together to form colonial states.

For decades Africans struggled to gain their independence. It was not until after World War II that the colonial territories became independent African states. Today, almost all of Africa is ruled by Africans. Large numbers of Africans live in modern cities. Rural Africa is also being transformed, and yet its people still engage in many of their customs and beliefs.

Contemporary circumstances and natural events have not always been kind to ordinary Africans. Today, however, new popular social movements and technological innovations pose great promise for future development.

George C. Bond, Ph.D., Director
Institute of African Studies
Columbia University, New York

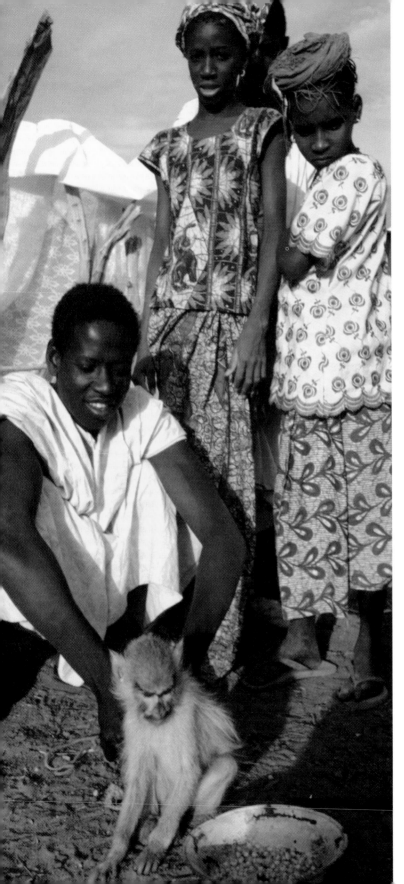

The Soninke
founded one
of Africa's
great empires,
the Empire of
Ghana.
Today they
live in many
parts of West
Africa.

chapter

1

THE PEOPLE

THROUGHOUT THEIR LONG HISTORY IN WEST Africa, the Soninke have been known by various names: the Soninke, Serakole, Sarakole, or Serahule. Some early Arab writers called them the Wakore or Wangara. The Soninke speak one of the languages of the Mande group. All of these languages are tonal. This means that a word may have a number of different meanings depending on whether it is pronounced with a high, middle, or low tone.

The Soninke have a proud history as the founders of the ancient Empire of Ghana. Ghana was the first great kingdom of medieval Africa. It was a landlocked empire of great size, power, and influence, built and managed by a West African people. Ancient Ghana should not be confused with the modern state of Ghana, which lies about 930 miles to the southeast of ancient Ghana. Modern Ghana is on the coast of the Atlantic Ocean. It was once called the Gold Coast, but took the name Ghana when it gained independence after British colonialism ended in 1957.

The Soninke were not the only people who lived in ancient Ghana, but they occupied controlling positions in the political, economic, and other aspects of life. The king himself was a Soninke. He was known as Kaya Magha, King of Gold. This title is still used by the Soninke.

Today, most Soninke live in the Republic of Mali. The customs and society of the present-day Soninke are not the same as those of the Empire of Ghana. However, they are rooted in history.

▼ MIGRATION ▼

The Soninke have a long history of migration. The Empire of Ghana was located at the southern edge of the Sahara Desert. This enabled the Soninke to prosper in trans-Saharan trade as farmers and as middlemen.

Today, the Soninke are widespread in West Africa and other parts of the world. Some Soninke live in Nigeria, where they have been successful in mining. The Soninke trade gold and kola nuts in the forest regions of modern Ghana, Burkina Faso, and Côte d'Ivoire. In Senegal, they produce and sell peanuts and

This map shows the Empire of Ghana, colored dark green. Trade also led to the creation of two later empires in this region: the empires of Mali and Songhay.

trade rice. In Mauritania, they farm and trade in gum. They are also economically successful in the modern Republic of Mali. The Bamana people of Mali use the name Maraka for the Soninke traders (who have adopted Bamana language and culture). In many other places Soninke traders are called *dyula* or *jula*, meaning "trader." Because of their profitable trading, the migrant Soninke are often wealthier than the people they live among.

Soninke communities are also found in

Mauritania, Cameroon, Zaire, Congo, Gabon, and the Central African Republic. In fact, they seem to be able to adapt and succeed almost anywhere. This is remarkable because the Soninke number only around 850,000 (about two-thirds of whom live in the Republic of Mali), and they are not the majority population group in any contemporary state in Africa.

▼ SLAVERY ▼

An explanation of Soninke business ability may be found in aspects of their history. Until the abolition of slavery the Soninke were a slave-raiding and slave-owning people. Most of their farming was done by slaves, so young Soninke men were free to pursue business opportunities elsewhere. Soninke aristocrats and free men owned most of the trade goods produced by the slaves. Some historians believe that some young Soninke males migrated all over the world to earn enough money to buy slaves.

After slavery was abolished at the end of the 1800s, Soninke trading patterns were forced to change. Soninke migrants began to buy many cattle. Some young Soninke men took low-paying jobs in Europe. They would use their wages to hire others to tend their cattle or farms at home. Thus many Soninke continued to migrate. Today, many of the French-speaking West Africans holding menial jobs in France are

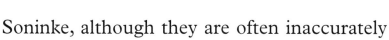

Soninke, although they are often inaccurately called Senegalese.

▼ SAILORS ▼

Working as crew members in European ships has long been an occupation of able-bodied Soninke men. When European merchants, especially the French, began to sail up the Niger and Senegal Rivers around 1850, the Soninke were the first people of the region to try to get hired by them. Known as *laptots*, Soninke sailors served in the French navy and on trading vessels. This work gave them opportunities to make international trade contacts. Many Soninke who settled in Europe and America before and shortly after World War II were former sailors.

Despite their migrations, most Soninke maintain strong links with their home communities. Many return there after a time, often enjoying a high standard of living based on what they have earned away from home.▲

The Empire of Ghana was built up through trade. Today, as in the past, camel caravans transport trade goods back and forth across the Sahara Desert.

chapter

2
THE LAND

ABOUT 2,000 YEARS AGO THE SONINKE LIVED
to the northwest of the great bend of the Niger
River, just south of the Sahara Desert. Some
writers even believe that Soninke communities
lived within the desert. Soninke territory
stretched from the Sahel in the north to the
edge of the savanna in the south.

The term Sahel comes from an Arabic word.
It means a shore, a port, or a stopping place
before or after a long journey. The Sahel was a
place where travelers and traders got ready to
set out on the risky journey across the Sahara to
North Africa and beyond. Those who had just
crossed the desert could rest there.

In recent times the Sahel has often been
drought-stricken. Once it had a mild climate
and plenty of grass for cattle to eat in the wet
season. However, herders did have to drive their

The savanna of West Africa is a grassland region with scattered trees. It provides grazing and is suitable for some farming.

cattle southward during the dry season in search of pasture.

The Soninke in the more southerly locations and those near rivers developed one of the earliest forms of farming in West Africa. This area is made up of grasslands with some scattered trees. It is called the savanna.

South of the savanna begins the forest belt. This region stretches along much of Africa's Atlantic coast.

These different climate and vegetation zones meant that nearby peoples could trade the items they produced with neighbors who offered different things in exchange.

▼ GROWTH OF TRADE ▼

The Soninke name for their ancient kingdom of Ghana was Wagadu. Wagadu took advantage of its location close to trade routes. From about 750 AD Wagadu became an important trading center. It was known for the trading of gold and ivory from the south, and salt from the desert to the north. The Soninke also sold food products to desert nomads. At the height of its power in the middle of the eleventh century, Ghana included much of Mali, Senegal, and Mauritania. Trade routes branched out from the capital at Kumbi Saleh. They linked the Empire of Ghana into a network of intercontinental trade.

Later, this set of factors that made Ghana great led to the rise of other similar empires in the region, including Mali and Songhay. Gold remained the key resource. Until Europeans reached the Americas, this region of Africa was Europe's major source of gold. Europeans bought their gold from the trans-Saharan traders. The Muslim world also used African gold to mint the coins they used for money. As Muslim groups began to compete with each other in the ninth and tenth centuries, each group wanted its own gold currency. This high demand for gold in Europe and the Muslim world made the miners and traders extremely wealthy.

It is estimated that hundreds of thousands of

The growth of trade and many cultural changes were due to the influence of Muslims. Here a Muslim prays, facing in the direction of the holy city of Mecca, while camels pass behind him.

Africans mined gold by hand to meet the demand. The mines in the forest regions were always kept secret from Muslim traders. Even when Muslims discovered and raided mines, they needed the miners to help them get the gold. It soon became clear to them that the trading business was the best way to be sure of a good supply of gold. In trade for gold, the Muslims offered things they valued little, like salt, cloth, and beads. The gold producers received trade goods they regarded as equal to the value of gold they exchanged. The rulers of Wagadu and the other empires that developed in this region placed a tax on gold and other things

Archaeologists have discovered the site that was most likely the capital of the Empire of Ghana, Kumbi Saleh. Seen here are the remains of a beautiful mosque.

produced in their countries. They also taxed every load of goods entering or leaving their territory.

For about 800 years the empires of this region, known as the Western Sudan, were among the wealthiest, strongest, and best organized states in the world. They were also great centers of learning and culture at a time when Europe was in what is called The Dark Ages. The growth of trade and culture in the Western Sudan was linked to the introduction of Islam.▲

chapter

3

HISTORY

NO ONE IS CERTAIN ABOUT THE EARLIEST history of the Soninke or exactly when their kingdom of Ghana was founded. What is known about these people in ancient times comes from Soninke oral tradition, archeology, and writings by Muslim scholars and travelers.

▼ SONINKE ORAL TRADITION ▼

According to oral tradition, the ancestor of the Soninke was a man named Dinga, who came from somewhere in the east. During Dinga's travels toward what would become the Empire of Ghana, he stopped in several places within the Sahel. He married many wives and had many children. These children became the founders of Soninke communities.

Even today the Soninke upper class, Wago, is made up of descendants of Dinga and his

BIDA THE SNAKE

According to Soninke legend, Dinga's son Dyabe made an agreement with Bida, a giant black snake, in order to settle at Kumbi. Bida demanded that a beautiful young woman be sacrificed to him once a year. All went well until a man killed Bida to save the woman he loved from being sacrificed. A curse of seven years' drought fell upon the Soninke as a result. The land dried up, there was nothing to eat, and the Soninke had to abandon Kumbi.

This story is not very helpful to historians in search of clear dates and facts. However, it suggests that for the Soninke belief in magical or spiritual beings and regular sacrifice were connected to the well-being of the state and the Soninke people.

warriors. The word Wagadu means the place where the Soninke Wago lived. Wagadu became another name for the Empire of Ghana.

▼ ARABIC CLUES ▼

The earliest written records of the Soninke are documents by Muslim scholars written around 790 AD, hundreds of years after the founding of Ghana. By that time Ghana was

The Empire of Ghana grew wealthy from gold mining. Today, mining continues in the Western Sudan in the same way as it has for more than a thousand years. Men work in tunnels (below). They fill containers with earth. Women and children haul the containers to the surface and wash out the gold (top).

already rich and strong, known as "the land of gold."

The early Soninke kings were called Ghana, which means "war chief" in Mande languages. By the time of written records in Arabic, the Soninke king is referred to as Kaya Magha, which means "King of Gold." This change in titles shows how the Soninke shifted from being most famous for their army to having control of trade.

The best picture we have of Ghana in Arabic writings is from Al-Bakri. He wrote in 1067. Thirteen years before this, the Almoravid Muslims of Ibn Yasin had invaded Ghana from the north and captured Aoudaghast, one of Ghana's important trading centers. Al-Bakri's information was thus both fresh and accurate. Also, Al-Bakri was based at Cordoba in Spain. The ruling Muslims there knew a great deal about the Western Sudan.

Al-Bakri described the great military strength of the emperor of Ghana, saying that he could command two hundred thousand warriors, including forty thousand archers. This force was far more powerful than European armies at that time. He mentioned that some Sudanese peoples were so desperate for salt, which was part of their diets, that they would trade it for its weight in gold. He also explained the emperor's system of tax on trade items, including copper, and on

Today, as in the past, salt is a major item of trade in the Western Sudan. This salt caravan is crossing the desert in Niger.

gold production. The emperor kept all the nuggets for himself; and others could deal only in gold dust.

To have become so wealthy, Ghana must have begun to form a trading city around 500 AD. Iron was probably important. It was used to make superior tools and weapons for use and trade. We know from oral history that there were many kings of Ghana before the Muslim era.

Al-Bakri mentions the captured city of Aoudaghast, and Kumbi Saleh, the capital of Ghana. Both were fine cities with impressive stone buildings. Al-Bakri reported that the capital was divided into two cities, six miles apart. One was the emperor's home and the other was a typical Muslim merchant city, containing twelve mosques.

Archaeologists digging at Kumbi Saleh have

Iron was probably a key factor in early Soninke history. Iron weapons enabled the Soninke to defeat others. Today, professional blacksmiths continue the ancient skills of working metal. These men are Soninke silversmiths in Senegal. They make jewelry and tools.

uncovered what they believe is Ghana's capital. It probably contained about 30,000 people. There were mosques and comfortable stone mansions. Many houses had two stories, and were rectangular. This style was favored throughout the Muslim world. In many of the walls were decorative niches or cavities. Surprisingly, almost no evidence of gold has been found, except for a horse's harness with gold details. However, it is clear that Kumbi Saleh was once a grand capital.

Al-Bakri described the emperor's part of the capital as a walled fortress. It contained several buildings with typical African cone-shaped roofs. Al-Bakri wrote: "Around the emperor's town are domed houses and shrines where the priests in charge of Soninke religion live and where the statues and tombs of their kings are. These groves are guarded; no one can enter them or see what they contain." Close to the emperor's palace were secret shrines and the tombs of past kings. The Soninke must have believed that worshiping their ancestors was very important.

The Soninke kings were probably thought of as holy. Visitors described two ways in which the emperor was treated as special: whenever he appeared his subjects fell on the ground and threw dust on their heads, and only he wore clothes of imported cloth.

Excavations have been carried out at Kumbi Saleh and other places that are associated with the early empires of West Africa. They help us develop a clearer picture of how grand these early African centers were. Seen here are the foundations of a mosque at Kumbi Saleh with supports for its columns, dated to about 1200 AD (above). Seen below are the remains of a house dated to about 1300 AD. Note the triangular niche set into the wall.

A VIEW OF THE EMPEROR

Al-Bakri gave a famous description of the emperor of Ghana at this time, Tunka Manin. In modern language, this is what witnesses reported:

When the emperor appears in public to hear and judge his people's complaints, he sits in a pavilion surrounded by horses dressed in gold cloth. Behind him are ten attendants holding shields and gold-handled swords. To his right are the princes of the empire, magnificently dressed and with gold braided into their hair. Seated on the ground in front of the emperor is the governor of the city, with the king's advisers seated on either side. The gate to the room is guarded by dogs of an excellent breed wearing collars made of silver and gold.

Al-Bakri also described the extraordinary burial of Soninke kings: "When the king dies, they build a huge wooden dome over the grave. They bring the king's body on a lightly covered bed and put him inside the dome. Alongside him they place his ornaments, weapons, and the eating and drinking vessels he used, filled with food and drink. Those who served him his food and drink are also put in. Then the door is closed and the dome is covered with mats and other materials. The people cover it with earth until it becomes a large mound, around which they dig a moat. Then sacrifices are made to the ancestors and offerings of beer."

Many mounds very similar to those described by Al-Bakri have been found by archaeologists in this region. This suggests that the early written reports were correct.

▼ ISLAM ▼

In spite of their long contact with the Islamic world, most of the Soninke still practiced their ancestral religion. The Soninke believed in many powerful spirits that had strong influences on the people and their fortunes. The ancestral spirits were revered because they had led the Soninke to the land they occupied. The ancestors remained interested in the well-being of their descendants. Dead kings were the most powerful ancestors of the Soninke.

The ancestors, as spirits, were important because they stood as the bridge between the spirit world and the human world, where they once lived. They were never very far from their living children. Although ancestors spoke the language of spirits, they were also able to speak the language of their people. Through special

Many Soninke today are Muslim. This small mosque is in the Soninke village of Hamdallaye Tessan in Senegal.

ceremonies the ancestors were persuaded to influence the spirit world in ways that would help their descendants.

Islam is based on belief in one almighty God, Allah. Thus Muslims opposed the Soninke religion that recognized many deities. Devout Muslims disliked the Soninke custom of greeting the king by pouring ashes and dust on their heads. This gave the impression that the Soninke saw him as divine and were thus worshiping beings other than Allah.

Such religious tension between Muslims and Soninke existed around the middle of the eleventh century when the Almoravids became a very important force in the history of the Soninke.

▼ THE ALMORAVIDS ▼

The Almoravids were Berbers, mostly of the Sanhaja clan. They were devout Muslims who

These Soninke Marabouts, or holy men, follow a strict interpretation of Islam.

combined a strict form of Islam with a desire for conquest. They began to concentrate their efforts on the Soninke region. Their activities reached a high point at the same time that their cattle-herding kinsmen were taking over Soninke farmland. In 1076 Ghana was defeated by the Almoravids. Within a decade the ruling Soninke group and a large number of the lower classes among the Soninke were converted to Islam.

▼ THE MARABOUTS ▼

In the 1800s Islamic scholars called Marabouts tried to make the Soninke take Islam more seriously. The Soninke were still not

31

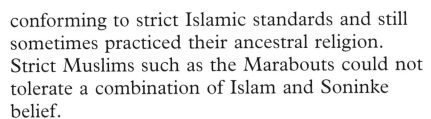

conforming to strict Islamic standards and still sometimes practiced their ancestral religion. Strict Muslims such as the Marabouts could not tolerate a combination of Islam and Soninke belief.

The Marabout wars to reform the Soninke continued until the mid-1800s. During the same time there were other groups trying to conquer the Soninke. Soon European colonialism was imposed on the whole area.

Although a small group of Soninke lived in the Gambia under British rule, most Soninke were colonized by the French.

▼ FRENCH COLONIALISM ▼

Before the French colonized the Senegal area, their influence began to be felt during the 1700s. The Soninke were already widely settled in this region. Their experience living in other parts of the world helped the Soninke to get along with the French and understand their culture.

Soninke *laptots* working on French boats in the 1800s spread French language and culture when they returned to their communities. Among peoples colonized by the French, any knowledge of French language and culture was an asset. Many of these returning Soninke therefore rose to high positions in traditional society. They were also used by the French to entrench colonialism. As chiefs they had great clout. They served as the link between their people and the colonial administrators. In return for their cooperation, the French gave them new privileges. For instance, members of their families were among the first to receive French education.

A major influence in recent Soninke history was the military policy in French West Africa. As drafted and volunteer soldiers in the colonial army, the Soninke were known as fierce fighters. Specific accounts of Soninke soldiers are few. They were lumped together with other groups in the Senegalese Rifles and later in the Sudanese Rifles. The Soninke fought for French colonialism in Africa, the Middle East, the Far East, and Indochina, later called Vietnam. Many Soninke served with distinction in the two World Wars. Their experiences changed their world views, and many of these soldiers moved to cities after the wars rather than return to their rural homes.

Today the Soninke seem more and more urban. However, Soninke tradition has not been completely destroyed. Urban and rural lifestyles among the Soninke are both important.

Colonialism caused a major change in the relationship between a Soninke and his or her village. In traditional society, each Soninke family had a certain rank in the village. The

Today, the Soninke continue to live in both rural and urban areas. However, rural lifestyles have changed a great deal in the last century. Seen above is a vegetable garden run by the women of Didé in Senegal. Below is a view of the town of Bakel in Senegal.

colonial government that was imposed on French West Africa changed the village—once the center of Soninke life—into a small part of a huge system. These villages and their people were no longer independent or self-sufficient.

Taxation and the end of slavery had a strong effect on the Soninke economy. Because they needed to pay taxes to the colonial government, Soninke men were forced to take on jobs to earn cash. The French always had big projects in development, especially building roads and railways. The few Soninke men left in the village to help with the farmwork were now called away to join colonial work groups. The neighboring people who might have taken their place as hired help were also out building for the colonial government.

French colonialism did not really affect Soninke religion, a mix of Islam and Soninke ancestral beliefs and practices. The French tried to convert them to Christianity. However, they could not convince the Soninke to change their spiritual beliefs.▲

Soninke farmers are busiest during the rainy season. A shared lunch provides
a welcome break for the men seen here.

chapter

4

TRADITION AND CUSTOMS

THE SONINKE BELIEVE THAT SPIRITS PROTECT them but can also cause them harm. Many of their religious ceremonies are based on this belief. Rituals are intended to praise and please the spirits so that they will bring good fortune. The acts and creatures of nature are believed to give signs that predict future events if they are read correctly.

The autumn is a time for many Soninke ceremonies. The chief of each family group sacrifices a bull at the west side of the village. This is done when the white egret and the stork have been seen migrating, which is a sure sign that winter is on the way. At this time of year the chiefs and aristocrats—those who can afford it—sacrifice fine animals to the spirits, hoping for prosperity in the new year. The fox and hyena are watched closely for signs: The new

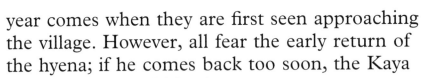

year comes when they are first seen approaching the village. However, all fear the early return of the hyena; if he comes back too soon, the Kaya Magha will die within the year.

The priest of a Soninke community is called the *gessere*. He is responsible for helping families and individuals carry out ceremonies that affect their private lives.

Many beautiful terracotta figures have been found close to the great bend in the Niger River. These four riders and one standing figure are about 750 years old. Their faces have special Soninke scarification marks on the temples.

▼ BIRTH ▼

Birth is, of course, the first sacred period in a person's life. To welcome a new baby to the world, the *gessere* gives it a little goat's milk. On its sixth day of life the infant's head is shaved by the priest, who gives the locks of hair to the mother. She keeps these until the child is a teenager, then gives them to him or her to wear as an amulet.

On a child's seventh day a name is chosen, and the *gessere* pierces the child's ear. The name is called out to the neighbors to give them the news, three times for a girl, four times for a boy. The priest recites the mother's and father's lineage. A person's ancestry is very

This wooden sculpture of a Soninke mother is about 700 years old.

important to the Soninke. Then it is time to prepare a feast. A bull is sacrificed, and neighbors come to wish the new parents well, bringing gifts of gold and hides to the festivities. Forty days after the naming ceremony, a silver or iron bracelet is placed on the child's left wrist, a special gift to welcome it into the world.

▼ INITIATION ▼

When a teenage boy can prove that he is responsible enough to take care of a horse by himself, he goes through an initiation ceremony to prepare him for adulthood. The initiation and circumcision period is a time of great importance for the whole community. Every few years many boys are initiated at once. Those who are ready are isolated in a hut in the woods. There they are taught correct adult behavior and the art of being a warrior. The elders also explain the various groups in society that the young men may try to join. These special groups require high entrance fees, and belonging to them is a sign of status. When the initiation period is over, the village celebrates with processions, gift-giving, and feasts, and the young men are ready for marriage.

▼ MARRIAGE ▼

Usually Soninke marriages are arranged by the families of the young people. Marriage is not

Many Soninke marriage customs are still followed today. This bride wears beautiful jewelry and expensive cloth that has been dyed with indigo, which makes blue shades. She has also put henna dye on her hands and feet.

only a union of two people, but a political and economic alliance of two families. Once a good match has been found, the *gessere* is sent to the potential bride's house. There he asks for her hand on behalf of the young man and offers gifts of gold and kola nuts to her family. This ceremony is repeated on three occasions; if the gifts are accepted all three times, the bride's family has accepted the groom.

The *gessere* then goes to the bride's parents, bearing more gifts along with the *tama*, a white cotton cloth over fifteen feet long, which officially marks the engagement. After presentation of the *tama*, the wedding takes place within eight days. The number eight is a reminder of pre-Islamic days, when the traditional Soninke week had eight days.

The bride appears at the groom's house dressed in blue and carrying a gourd. At her new home, she bathes and changes into a white dress. Her maid or friend makes a porridge of sorghum and distributes it in the bride's gourd to the guests. This is symbolic of a taboo that the bride must observe: she can eat only sorghum porridge for a year. At the end of that time, a feast is held called "leaving the porridge." The wife cooks a meal of mutton and beer for her husband's father. After this she can eat these foods herself and is finally considered part of her new family.

It was once common for Soninke men to have several wives, if they could afford it. Today, men often prefer to have only one wife. This family is from Mauritania.

One aspect of Soninke tradition that works in harmony with Islam is polygyny, or having more than one wife at a time. The Soninke ancestor Dinga had several wives, as did his son Dyabe. Multiple marriages were probably common in ancient times. It is now certainly the preferred practice among the Soninke. Islamic law allows a man to marry up to four wives provided he loves and treats them all equally. This form of marriage increases the size of the family and the number of workers. More laborers bring more wealth and increase the influence of the head of

43

At wedding ceremonies, everyone wears their finest outfit. This Soninke couple is returning from a wedding.

the family. But polygyny promotes rivalry and competition among a man's wives, and this can be difficult for the parents and the children.

▼ THE DISPLAY OF WEALTH ▼

Soninke tradition and custom encourage the public display of wealth, and this encourages competition for status and power. Marriage ceremonies provide excellent opportunities for families to show their affluence and superiority over their rivals. Such occasions also make rivals more determined to become wealthier. Even when they are married, daughters of wealthy

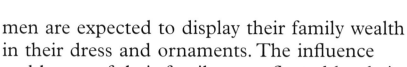

men are expected to display their family wealth in their dress and ornaments. The influence and honor of their family are reflected by their appearance.

Processions are another important way to display wealth. The adoption of Islam has discouraged processions and the masked dances that follow them, but they still take place. Old traditions still govern what kind of masks are worn by certain classes of society. Hooded masks are worn by those of lowest birth; wooden masks, by those of higher rank. The highest notables may be recognized in a procession by their golden masks.

The aristocrats among the Soninke acquired and increased their wealth through plunder and trade in gold, slaves, salt, cereals, and cattle. They also used political power. Today, much of the wealth comes from farming, family members working abroad, commercial activities, and real estate. ▲

5
SOCIETY

SONINKE COMMUNITIES ARE ORGANIZED around the male members of the various families. In the family the father exercises great power. Within each family or group the oldest male wields authority over the other members. Together these elders act as rulers of the entire community. This type of rulership has great respect for the wisdom of old age. Because they are the oldest men in the community, the elders are nearest the ancestors. This makes them best qualified to transmit the traditions of the ancestors to the younger generations.

Soninke society is marked by constant competition and rivalry between communities. Even within the communities there is rivalry between chiefs. This has become an important aspect of Soninke tradition.

Male elders play a leading role in Soninke society. These men are seated on a special raised bench.

▼ TRADITIONAL HIERARCHY ▼

Despite the rivalry among groups and individuals in Soninke society, the people still try to live within the traditional ranking system. The population is organized according to clearly known levels of social status. Each level of Soninke society has certain rights and privileges and duties and obligations.

The population can be divided into seven groups. The first and most privileged group is the king's family and descendants of the founding fathers. Next in status and influence are the warlords' descendants. In the next group are the free farmers, who may be forced to work for the aristocrats. They can also be taxed.

The fourth group consists of descendants of people who converted to Islam when most of the

47

population were still practicing only Soninke religion. Because these early converts separated themselves by accepting Islam, they were denied the right to serve as warriors or to become chiefs. Their descendants still follow that tradition. The closest they can get to political power is to become clients of powerful aristocrats. They are, however, good traders. The most learned Soninke Muslim scholars are members of this group.

The fifth status group is made up of the poor. All people who joined the community as immigrants are considered a part of this group. They do not have privileges because they cannot trace their relationship to a Soninke ancestor.

The artisans form the sixth group. Although they may be wealthy, these people have low status and are not allowed to marry outside their group. The artisans include the praise singers—*griots*—who are experts in Soninke history.

Slaves once made up the last and least privileged group in the society. In theory, slaves could buy their freedom; however, few slaves could find the money. Even worse, if the slave was married he was expected to buy his wife's freedom as well. Finally, the master had to be willing to let the slave go.

Around 1850 slaves made up at least one-third of the population of the Soninke. It also seems that most of these slaves were women.

Although artisans, such as this weaver, have low status, they may be very wealthy.

The slave trade was ended in these parts of Africa toward the end of the 1800s. Demands by Africans, economic forces, as well as the policies of French colonialism combined to end the inhuman practice. After they were freed, many former slaves stayed on at the households of their former owners, working as paid labor.

Slaves were not quiet and passive throughout the history of the Soninke. Early history provides records of slave revolts. It was not until the end of the 1800s, however, that the revolts seemed to threaten traditional society. By about 1910 most slaves had established lives on their own. Nowadays, in spite of the strength of tradition among the Soninke, descendants of

49

The Soninke are widely scattered throughout West Africa. This man in Mauritania, standing beside his unusual luggage, waits for his airplane flight.

slaves have grown more vocal in matters that concern the whole population.

▼ DAILY LIFE ▼

The Soninke are spread over a large area of West Africa and beyond. Their communities are found within countries dominated by other peoples. Over a long period, they have learned to be adaptable. In some environments, such as among the Bamana of Mali, they have adapted so well that they blend into the population. Because of this trait, the daily life of the Soninke varies greatly from one community to another.

Soninke lifestyle is also affected by the high level of migration of young males. Most of these migrants eventually return to their communities, bringing all sorts of new ideas and a great deal of wealth that alters lifestyles.

Most Soninke still live in villages, although many people migrate to the cities and elsewhere. The village is, therefore, the main environment in which the Soninke carry on their political, social, and economic activities. Often it is organized around one main status group that identifies the village. There are royal villages, aristocratic villages, villages for artisans, and so on. Slave villages are rare. When slavery was abolished, the slaves also began to migrate.

Though they are credited with founding the great Empire of Ghana, today the Soninke are not connected by one central government.

Within the village, local government consists of the elders from several families. The oldest of these elders presides. Within the family, the elder not only controls the members but also serves as a link between them and the village. There is constant competition among the

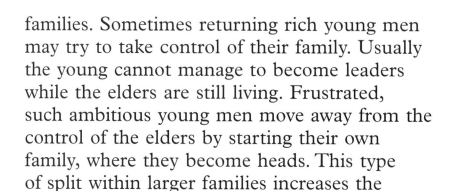

families. Sometimes returning rich young men may try to take control of their family. Usually the young cannot manage to become leaders while the elders are still living. Frustrated, such ambitious young men move away from the control of the elders by starting their own family, where they become heads. This type of split within larger families increases the rivalry and competition in the daily life of the Soninke.

In addition to government by elders of the family, age-grades are also important among the Soninke. Age-grades bring together youths of specific age ranges and give them a forum for handling problems that concern them directly. They allow youths from various families to meet and work together. The day-to-day management of age-grades is handled by the oldest of the youths of high status. The cooking and serving of meals and the cleaning up are done by youths of the lowest social groups.

The Soninke are very conscious of status and honor. The aristocrats despise farming, seeing it as a lowly occupation. However, they need wealth from the land to sustain their status, so they hire others to farm for them. Because of migration, many potential farm workers are away from their native villages. To compensate, these travelers send money home to hire workers from neighboring communities. In addition to

Rural Soninke houses often have artistic designs on the outside and inside, as seen in these examples from Mauritania.

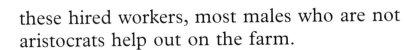

these hired workers, most males who are not aristocrats help out on the farm.

▼ FARMING ▼

Elders give farmlands to male members of the family and, occasionally, women. Before any individual receives land, a large plot is first set aside as a family farm.

Each family head goes to the farm most days of the week with his sons and hired workers. After lunch the sons are free to work their individual farms for the rest of the day. Younger brothers may work for their older siblings for a few hours after lunch before going to their own farms. It is the duty of the head of the family to feed the workers.

Soninke society expects men to do certain jobs and women to do others. Men grow cotton and cereals such as millet, sorghum, and maize. Women concentrate on peanuts, rice, and indigo. Although Soninke women play important roles in the family, very few actually own farmland. Whatever women produce on their farms belongs to them after they have supplied family food needs. Women's farming tasks are sowing seeds, weeding, tending, and fending off birds and other destructive animals. They also help with harvesting. Women have a more important role in the Soninke community when men are migrating to other regions.▲

Today, the Soninke have many farming projects. Often, they are run by women or men working together. Fishing is another important community activity.

chapter

6

A VIEW OF THE FUTURE

THE SONINKE CAN FACE THE FUTURE WITH confidence. With their historical background, geographical location, and experience in commerce and in living with other peoples, they have good prospects in a changing world.

In ancient times the Soninke traded with the Berber and Arab world and learned about North Africa and Europe. Their commercial routes also brought them into contact with most of West Africa.

Later contact with British and French colonialism opened up more of the world to the Soninke. Many migrated to Europe. Migration has strengthened Soninke knowledge of the world and helped to develop Soninke home communities.

Adherence to Islam has also improved the future of these people. Islam unites them with

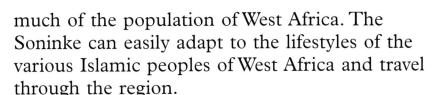

much of the population of West Africa. The Soninke can easily adapt to the lifestyles of the various Islamic peoples of West Africa and travel through the region.

The Soninke have remained attached to their ancestral roots. They adapted their new religion so that it mixed with their traditional culture. For centuries, the Soninke have been considering new ideas from the viewpoint of their own traditions. Because of this skill, they are not in danger of losing their traditions even when they come under foreign influence. *Griots* play an important role in preserving traditions by telling historical stories. Proverbs and folktales communicate Soninke attitudes. On the other hand, the Soninke have also been flexible enough to drop practices like slavery in favor of better ideas or methods of doing things.

The key to the Soninke future may be their ability to make a living under any circumstances. Wherever these people have lived, they have worked hard to improve their position. For centuries they have been involved in long-distance and even dangerous economic ventures. They have been able to adapt to changing patterns of trade. There is hardly a profitable product in which the Soninke have not traded. More recently, they have also become active in real estate investment in cities such as Dakar in Senegal and Bamako in Mali.

THE HYENA AND THE HARE

Once the Hyena and the Hare challenged each other.

Hare said, "Let's each go home following whichever road we choose. We'll see who comes home in the best shape." Hyena chose a smooth road with no bushes to climb over. Hare chose a rugged road with sticks and bushes everywhere, which made Hyena laugh.

When Hyena was out of sight, Hare pulled out his drum and began to beat a dance rhythm, calling

Kennu wa ri o n canga, pere pere, kennu xari o n canga!

Come, guinea fowl, come! We want you to amuse us!

Suddenly a group of guinea fowl swooped down from a tree and began to dance to the drumbeat. The Hare hit one on the head with his drumstick and put it in his hunting bag. The other birds cried, "Oh, who has killed our pretty guinea fowl?" They looked around, but the Hare had hidden behind one of the many bushes along the path, so the birds gave up and flew into the trees.

Later along the path the Hare began to beat his drum again. Again the guinea fowl came when he called and danced in dizzying circles to the beat. Hare hit another bird on the head and put that one in his bag, then ran and hid until the fowl had stopped looking for him.

When Hare got home, he had two fine guinea fowl in his sack, which his wife made into a delicious supper. When Hyena got home, he was empty-handed, and his wife was angry. "You good-for-nothing!" she said. "Where have you been? Mr. and Mrs. Hare are eating like royalty tonight, and we have no supper." Hyena was confused and went to check on Hare. He saw their beautiful dinner and tried once again to outsmart his rival.

"Say, old Hare," he began, "I'll tell you what. If you teach me how to get guinea fowl like these, I'll show you how to make the best sauce in the country." Hare was a nice fellow, and he loved good sauces, so he showed Hyena how to play the drum, call the fowl, and hit one on the head with his stick.

Feeling very smug, Hyena tripped off into the woods. He began to beat the dance rhythm that Hare had taught him, calling

Kennu wa ri o n canga, pere pere, kennu xari o n canga!

Come, guinea fowl, come! We want you to amuse us!

Sure enough, along came the guinea fowl and began their crazy dance. Hyena got very excited and struck out at two fowl. Both fell unconscious, and the greedy Hyena gobbled them up right there in the path, everything but the feathers. The other birds watched in horror and spread the news to all the forest fowl not to come when Hyena called them.

You can bet he was in trouble when he got home!

SONINKE PROVERBS

Senlenmen we wurunu za tigiyen leneono garihan ya di.
A young colt can run fast, but only an experienced horse
    can handle a rough road.

*An do sere gabe ra wa yi yaage jin mini, tudu jin ga na ri i wo
    wurunu an wa.*
Many people will help you drink honey, but when there is
    something bitter to swallow everyone runs away.

Haare sire nta dangini tiiden di katti kanmun wa.
There is no one better than smoke to send as a messenger
    to the sky.

*Sere we gede soxono lenki n'a wara xunbanne daxun
    kaane.*
Dig a well today for tomorrow's thirst.

*Xirisen digamen ga na dalla gunnen de moxo-moxo a nta
    wuyini nenea abada.*
Some people believe that the wise words of the elders get
    lost in the bush, but they always return to the village.

Sometimes economic success makes the
Soninke the target of dislike and distrust in their
host community. When the economy is bad,
people tend to look for scapegoats. Often the
blame is placed on foreigners.

The Soninke have been fortunate in many
ways. Over the centuries they have learned to
survive and flourish. With their background,

The Soninke are proud of their rich history. The remains of Kumbi Saleh, seen here, are evidence of their early achievements.

experience, and understanding of the world, most Soninke view the future with optimism while preserving a proud memory of their past.▲

Glossary

Almoravid Muslims Political and religious group of Berbers who spearheaded the spread of Islam among the Soninke.

Berbers Large North African ethnic group inhabiting present-day Algeria, Morocco, Tunisia, Mauritania, and parts of the Sahara Desert.

dyula Name for traders from the western parts of West Africa.

griots Traditional oral historians and praise singers.

Kaya Magha "King of Gold," a title of the Soninke king.

laptots West Africans serving with the French fleet on the Senegal River.

Marabouts Members of Islamic intellectual and military groups.

polygyny Practice of having more than one wife at a time.

sorghum Edible grain or cereal.

Wago Collective term for the class of society that includes the king and aristocrats.

For Further Reading

Boahen, Adu. *Topics in West African History.* London: Longman, 1986.

Buah, F. K. *West Africa Since A.D. 1000*, Bk. 1. London: Macmillan, 1977.

Chou, Daniel, and Skinner, Elliott. *A Glorious Age in Africa: The Story of Three Great African Empires.* Trenton: African World Press, 1990.

Harris, Joseph E. *Africans and Their History.* New York: New American Library, 1972.

Koslow, Philip. *Ancient Ghana: The Land of Gold.* New York: Chelsea House Publishers, 1995.

McKissick, Patricia and McKissick, Frederick. *The Royal Kingdoms of Ghana, Mali and Songhay: Life in Medieval Africa.* New York: Henry Holt, 1994.

Osae, T. A., and Nwabara, S. N. *A Short History of West Africa, A.D. 1000–1800.* Bk. 1. London: Hodder & Stoughton, 1980.

Shinnie, Margaret. *Ancient African Kingdoms.* New York: New American Library, 1965.

Stride, G. T., and Ifeka, C. *People and Empires of West Africa.* London: Thomas Nelson, 1977.

Index

ABOUT THE AUTHOR

C. Onyeka Nwanunobi holds a B.A. with honors in History from the University of Nigeria, Nsukka, and an M.A. and a Ph.D. from the University of Toronto. He has taught at both places and is presently in the Department of Anthropology at the University of Toronto. He has published in Africa, Europe, and North America.

PHOTO CREDITS

Cover, pp. 8, 16, 34 bottom, 36, 43, 47, 49, 53, 55 © Alex de Sherbanin; p. 14 © M. Ascari/Gamma Liaison International; p. 18 © W. Gartung/Gamma Liaison International; pp. 19, 27, 60 © Serge Robert; p. 22 © Gilles Coulon/Gamma Liaison International; p. 24 © Mike Foster/National Geographic; pp. 25, 30, 31, 34 top, 41 © Andrew F. Clark; pp. 38, 39 courtesy of Bernard de Grunne; pp. 44, 50 © Sarah Hughes.

CONSULTING EDITOR
Gary N. van Wyk, Ph.D.

LAYOUT AND DESIGN
Kim Sonsky